Junior High Bible Study Series

My Family Life

Group's R.E.A.L. Guarantee to you:
This Group resource incorporates our R.E.A.L. approach to ministry—one that encourages long-term retention and life transformation. It's ministry that's:

Relational
Because learner-to-learner interaction enhances learning and builds Christian friendships.

Experiential
Because what learners experience through discussion and action sticks with them up to 9 times longer than what they simply hear or read.

Applicable
Because the aim of Christian education is to equip learners to be both hearers and doers of God's Word.

Learner-based
Because learners understand and retain more when the learning process takes into consideration how they learn best.

My Family Life

Junior High Bible Study Series

Copyright © 2004 Group Publishing, Inc.

All rights reserved. No part of this book may be reproduced in any manner whatsoever without prior written permission from the publisher, except where noted in the text and in the case of brief quotations embodied in critical articles and reviews. For information, write Permissions, Group Publishing, Inc., Dept. PD, P.O. Box 481, Loveland, CO 80539.

Visit our Web site: **www.grouppublishing.com**

Credits
Contributing Authors: Jan Kershner, Erin McKay, Julie Meiklejohn, and Michael D. Warden
Editors: Tammy L. Bicket and Dawn M. Brandon
Acquisitions Editor: Kelli B. Trujillo
Creative Development Editor: Amy Simpson
Chief Creative Officer: Joani Schultz
Copy Editor: Patty Wyrick
Art Director: Jane Parenteau
Print Production Artist: Joyce Douglas
Illustrator: Matt Wood
Cover Art Director/Designer: Jeff A. Storm
Cover Photographer: Daniel Treat
Production Manager: DeAnne Lear

Unless otherwise noted, Scripture taken from the HOLY BIBLE, NEW INTERNATIONAL VERSION®. Copyright © 1973, 1978, 1984 by International Bible Society. Used by permission of Zondervan Publishing House. All rights reserved.

ISBN 0-7644-2496-3
10 9 8 7 6 5 4 3 2 1   13 12 11 10 09 08 07 06 05 04
Printed in the United States of America.

Table of Contents

4 · Introduction

**6 · Study 1: Blessed Be the Ties:
How to Really Love Your Family**
   The Point: God is pleased when family members love each other.
   Scripture Source: 1 Corinthians 13:4-7

**14 · Study 2: "My Teenagers Just
Don't Understand Me!"**
   The Point: As a Christian, you should treat your parents with respect and love.
   Scripture Source: 1 Corinthians 13:11-13   Ephesians 5:1-2; 6:1-3

**25 · Study 3: Honoring Your Parents–
No Matter What**
   The Point: God wants you to honor your parents.
   Scripture Source: Exodus 20:12   2 Samuel 13:1–18:18
                     1 Kings 2:1–4:34   Proverbs 6:20-23

38 · Study 4: Why Can't We Just Get Along?
   The Point: Through God's love, your brothers and sisters can be your friends.
   Scripture Source: Genesis 37:17-28   Numbers 12:1-9
                     Luke 10:38-42   Ephesians 4:1-3
                     Hebrews 13:1   1 Peter 3:8-9
                     1 John 4:19-21   Matthew 5:23-24; 12:46-50;
                                        18:15, 21-22

47 · Changed 4 Life

My Family Life

Families are a wonderful gift from God. They make our own existence possible. They nurture us, teach us, provide for us, protect us, and give us our start in life. A good family can give teenagers the positive self-image and solid foundation they need to conquer the world as adults. But not all families are so positive. A destructive family can do more damage to a person than any other person or institution.

It's important to note that most teenagers aren't all that sure where their own family falls on the spectrum of good to bad. Chances are, this is the only family situation your students have ever experienced. It's hard to know what's normal, what's good, and what's part of the growing process when they have no other experiences with which to compare their own families. That's why it's so important for teenagers to talk about what they are experiencing and struggling with in their own families. God's Word has a lot to say about families. *My Family Life* will help your teenagers learn to see their families realistically and will give them practical tools to improve and make the most of their family life.

In the first study, teenagers will learn the most basic truth of all about families—family members should love each other. Your students will discover and commit to specific ways they can improve their relationships with family members.

In the second study, students will learn that their parents need their respect and love. They'll see Mom and Dad in a new light and discover new reasons to obey them, treat them respectfully, and help make their difficult jobs a little easier.

In the third study, teenagers will be introduced to the concept that God's commandment to honor their parents is non-negotiable. No matter how parents may fail or disappoint us, we're still responsible to honor them. Students will learn practical ways they can honor their parents—regardless of how their parents treat them.

In the fourth study, teenagers will turn their attention to those amazing friends and annoying irritants—brothers and sisters. No matter how close a family is, siblings have trouble getting along at times. This session reminds students that despite their differences, their brothers and sisters can be their friends.

These are crucial studies that can greatly impact every teenager you teach. As you lead these sessions, pray for your students and their families every day. Get to know your students' families and individual family situations so you can tailor the truths of this study to most effectively meet each junior higher's needs. Remember your own life experiences and how you felt about your family when you were in junior high, and get ready to see your students changed for life!

My Family Life will help your teenagers learn to see their families realistically and will give them practical tools to improve and make the most of their family life.

junior high bible study series
About Faith 4 Life™

Use Faith 4 Life studies to show your teenagers how the Bible is relevant to their lives. Help them see that God can invade every area of their lives and change them in ways they can only imagine. Encourage your students to go deeper into faith—faith that will sustain them for life! Faith 4 Life, forever!

Faith 4 Life™: Junior High Bible Study Series helps young teenagers take a Bible-based approach to faith and life issues. Each book in the series contains these important elements:

- ■ **Life application of Bible truth**—Faith 4 Life studies help teenagers understand what the Bible says and then apply that truth to their lives.

- ■ **A relevant topic**—Each Faith 4 Life book focuses on one main topic, with four studies to give your students a thorough understanding of how the Bible relates to that topic. These topics were chosen by youth leaders as the ones most relevant for junior high-age students.

- ■ **One point**—Each study makes one point, centering on that one theme to make sure students really understand the important truth it conveys. This point is stated upfront and throughout the study.

- ■ **Simplicity**—The studies are easy to use. Each contains a "Before the Study" box that outlines any advance preparation required. Each study also contains a "Study at a Glance" chart so that you can quickly and easily see what supplies you'll need and what each study will involve.

- ■ **Action and interaction**—Each study relies on experiential learning to help students learn what God's Word has to say. Teenagers discuss and debrief their experiences in large groups, small groups, and individual reflection.

- ■ **Reproducible handouts**—Faith 4 Life books include reproducible handouts for students. No need for student books!

- ■ **Tips, tips, and more tips**—Faith 4 Life studies are full of "FYI" tips for the teacher, providing extra ideas, insights into young people, and hints for making the studies go smoothly.

- ■ **Flexibility**—Faith 4 Life studies include optional activities and bonus activities. Use a study as it's written, or use these options to create the study that works best for your group.

- ■ **Follow-up ideas**—At the end of each book, you'll find a section called "Changed 4 Life." This section provides ideas for following up with your students to make sure the Bible truths stick with them.

Study 1

Blessed Be the Ties: How to Really Love Your Family

RELATIONSHIPS

restored

"**Y**ou *will* clean your room...and I don't want to hear another word about it!"

"I don't want to clean my room!"

"Do it *now*!"

As teenagers reach adolescence, power struggles within families seem to be the norm rather than the exception. Teenagers are seeking independence and autonomy from their parents, while parents want to protect and nurture their teenagers. It sometimes seems that teenagers don't want to have anything to do with their families, but they need their families' love and support.

In our families, we should learn, grow, and give and receive unconditional love. But teenagers may not know what that means.

This study will help teenagers identify and examine different components of love and how those components fit into their own family relationships. Teenagers will discover and commit to specific ways they can improve their own relationships with family members.

The Study at a Glance

Warm-Up (10-15 minutes)

Meet Your Family!
What students will do: Perform family-situation skits with their new "families."
Needs: ❏ slips of paper   ❏ pencils
❏ 2 coffee cans

Bonus Activity (10-15 minutes)
What students will do: Focus on what's lovable about their family members.
Needs: ❏ 5 chenille craft wires for each student

Bible Connection (25-30 minutes)

Love My Family as Myself?
What students will do: Travel with their families, explore 1 Corinthians 13:4-7, and apply what they learn to their relationships with family members.
Needs: ❏ Bibles   ❏ scissors
❏ tape   ❏ newsprint
❏ markers   ❏ pencils
❏ paper   ❏ "Family—What's Really Important?" handouts (p. 13)

Life Application (10-15 minutes)

Love You Can See
What students will do: Apply what they've learned about expressing love to family members by sharing a special snack, and commit to showing love to their family members.
Needs: ❏ ingredients and supplies for banana splits (or another snack)
❏ index cards
❏ pencils

The Point

▶ God is pleased when family members love each other.

Scripture Source

1 Corinthians 13:4-7
Paul describes "the most excellent way" of love.

Before the Study

For the "Love My Family as Myself?" activity, you'll need to set up three separate stations that are close together enough for minimal travel time but far apart enough for teenagers to work without distraction. Photocopy the "Family—What's Really Important?" handout (p. 13), and cut apart the three sections. Tape each station's instructions to the floor or to a wall at the station. For Station 1, set out several large sheets of newsprint and plenty of markers. For Station 3, set out paper and pencils.

Warm-Up

Meet Your Family!

(10 to 15 minutes)

As teenagers arrive, give each person two slips of paper and a pencil.

SAY:

■ Today we're going to discuss how the way family members treat each other can be a blessing. To start, I'd like you to write your name on one of the slips of paper I gave you. On the other slip of paper, write a sentence or two describing a situation that involves a family. It can be either a good situation or a bad situation. For example, you could write about a family arguing over pizza toppings or a family celebrating Thanksgiving together. Make sure your sentences tell who was involved, what happened, where and when it happened, and why you think it happened.

Give teenagers a few minutes to write, and then have them put the slips with their names on them in one coffee can and the situation slips in the other can.

SAY:

■ Now it's your job to show us some of these situations. I'll draw one of the situations out of the can, and then I'll draw several names out of the other can. The people whose names I draw will form a group, and I'll tell you the role each of you will be playing in the situation. Groups will then have three minutes to create brief skits demonstrating their situations.

Draw names and situations, then assign roles within each situation. Have teenagers form groups to prepare their skits.

> In this activity, teenagers will be forming groups they will "travel" with throughout the rest of the study. Groups should have between three and five people, so you'll need to figure out roughly how many people to include in each situation skit group before you start drawing names. You may need to adapt some of the situations to fit the number of people you need in each group.

As you draw names and situations, assign each person a role within the family, such as mom, dad, older brother, and so on. You may want to adapt a few situations in order to create a few nontraditional families, such as single-parent families or families that comprise children living with grandparents.

After five minutes, call time and have groups present their skits. Lead teenagers in applauding each team's efforts. After students have finished, have them answer the following questions within their groups, then have volunteers share their teams' answers with the class.

ASK:
- How do you feel about the way the members of your family treated each other?
- How should members of any family treat each other?
- Should family members treat each other differently, depending on the situation they're in? Explain.

SAY:
- Today we're going to discuss how family members should

The Point ▶ treat each other. We're going to discover why <u>God is pleased when family members love each other</u>, and we're going to find some real, valuable ways we can show love to our family members—whatever our situations are. For the rest of the study, the people in your skit group will be your "family."

✱ Bonus Activity ✱

(10 to 15 minutes)
If you have time, try this additional activity after "Meet Your Family!"

Give each student five chenille craft wires, and instruct them to bend the wires into "Family Focus" eyeglasses. Bend two wires into heart shapes to form the rims. Use one wire as the bridge to connect the two rims and the remaining two as earpieces. Have students form pairs (or trios) to try to look more clearly at each member of their real-life families. Students should consider each family member, looking specifically for qualities, attitudes, and actions that make him or her lovable. The purpose of having a partner (or two) is that often others can see those close to us more clearly than we can. Realizing that their parents aren't so strict or that their sister isn't bossier than anyone else's can help teenagers see their families in a more favorable light.

SAY:
- **Your job as partners is to find things to love and appreciate about each member of your families. Help each other out. Use your powerful "Family Focus" glasses to focus on some things your parents, brothers, and sisters do, are, don't do, say, don't say, and so on that are worth loving and appreciating. Take seven minutes and see how many things to love you can come up with about each member of your family.**

When time is up, bring students back together, and lead a discussion about their changed focus on their families.

ASK:
- What new things did you find to love about your parents?
- What new things did you find to love about your brothers and sisters?
- How did your partner see your family differently than you did?
- How did what you heard about your partner's family make you see your own family differently?
- How similar was your perspective of your family and your partner's perspective of his or her family? Did that surprise you? Explain.

SAY:
- God is pleased when family members love each other. ◀ **The Point** Sometimes it seems harder than it should be because of our perspective. We focus on the negative things that bug us and fail to focus on the things our family members do well. When we deliberately focus on the good things instead of the bad, it's a whole lot easier to love our families.

This would be a great study in which to get your teenagers' family members involved! Involving family members creates shared experiences and is a great way to open or improve communication. If you decide to invite family members, encourage them to participate fully in all of the activities.

It's possible that some students in your group may be in negative-even abusive-family situations. The concept of loving members of their families may be very difficult, confusing, and painful. Be sensitive to teenagers' reactions to this study, and offer to talk privately with any student. Remember that you may have a legal responsibility to report suspected abuse to official authorities. **FYI**

Love My Family as Myself?

(25 to 30 minutes)

Bible Connection

SAY:
- For the next part of the study, you'll be traveling with your family group to three different stations. Follow the instructions at each station, and complete the tasks as a family. In your family, choose one person to be in charge of reading the directions and another person to ensure that everyone is involved in all the tasks at each station. You'll have about twenty minutes to complete the three stations. I'll tell you when to switch to another station.

Point out where the stations are located. Assign a fairly even number of groups to each station.

> You may want to recruit an adult volunteer to help at each station. If you're not able to recruit volunteers, you can tailor the activity to fit the maturity level of your teenagers. Depending on the size of your group, you may want to complete each station activity together.

After about seven minutes, have groups move to their next stations. After another seven minutes, have teenagers move again. After a final seven minutes, have teenagers come back together in one big group.

SAY:

- You've had a chance to examine what the Bible says about the way people should treat each other. The words of 1 Corinthians 13 can apply especially to families.

ASK:

- After completing these activities, why do you think family members should love each other?
- Is loving family members easy? Explain.
- **The Point ▶** Why do you think <u>a family's love pleases God</u>?
- What's one thing you learned about how you can show love to your family?

Life Application: Love You Can See

(10 to 15 minutes)

SAY:

- One of the most important ways we can show love to our family members is by serving them—by trying to see their needs and meeting them without being asked.

ASK:

- What are some ways you could serve the members of your family?

SAY:

- We're going to put this idea into practice with our family groups now.

On a large table, set out the ingredients and supplies to make banana splits (or another snack), and explain that one family at a time will go to the table and make banana splits for each other.

SAY:

- You'll need to serve each other—no one can serve himself or herself. One other thing: No one in the family may talk. You'll need to watch one another to determine each other's needs. I'll tell each family when to get the snack. After you have your snack, you may sit back down with your family and enjoy it.

Hand out index cards and pencils, and

SAY:

- While one family's members are serving each other, I'd like the rest of you to think about the different ways of showing love to family members that we talked about today. Choose one way of showing love that you feel you can commit to during this week, and write it on your card. For example, you might write, "I'll show love by helping my little brother with his homework" or "I'll show love by not arguing with my mom when she asks me to do something."

Have one family at a time make snacks for each other until all the groups have their snacks. Then

SAY:

- Today we've examined why <u>God is pleased when family members love each other</u>, and we've discussed practical ways to show love to our family members. I'd like us to close in prayer. I'll begin the prayer, and then we'll have a few moments of silence in which you can ask God to help you keep the commitment you wrote down. Then I'll close the prayer.

◀ **The Point**

Begin the prayer by saying: **Dear God, thank you for families. Please help us to show love to our family members...**

Allow a few moments for teenagers to pray in silence, and then close the prayer. Remind teenagers to take their commitment cards home with them.

One excellent way to help build, preserve, and improve your teenagers' family relationships is to plan events that involve the whole family. Adolescents and their parents often have trouble communicating. But events that can bring them together on neutral ground while helping them to have fun together may go a long way toward improving family communication. Here are some ideas for family events:

- a parent-youth retreat
- a parent-youth discussion panel
- family game nights
- a family missions trip
- an "oldies but goodies" night in which parents share their favorite music with their teenagers
- seminars for teenagers about getting along with parents
- seminars for parents about getting along with their teenagers, such as *Parenting Teenagers for Positive Results* by Jim Burns (available from Group Publishing, Inc.)
- parent guest speakers

For more fun ideas that involve the whole family, see *Family-Friendly Ideas Your Church Can Do* (Group Publishing, Inc., 1998).

Family
What's *Really* Important?

STATION 1

Read 1 Corinthians 13:4 as a group, and follow the instructions below.

1. Take turns answering these questions in your group:
   - Which characteristic in this verse do you find easiest to practice with your family members?
   - Which characteristic do you find most difficult?

2. As a group, choose one of the characteristics. Use the newsprint and markers to create a banner that shows (or tells) ways you can use the characteristic to show love to your own family members. Make sure that everyone's ideas are included and that everyone has a part in creating the banner. Keep your completed banner with you.

   At the leader's instruction, move to Station 2. Be sure to leave this sheet here.

STATION 2

As a group, read 1 Corinthians 13:5 and follow the instructions below.

1. Take turns sharing about a family situation in which you had a difficult time with one of the characteristics in this verse. For example, you might tell about a time you got really mad at your brother because he got to watch what he wanted to on TV.

2. Take turns completing the following sentences within your group:
   - I get angry at a member of my family when...
   - When I get angry, I act...
   - To express love instead of anger at a family member, I could...

   At the leader's instruction, move to Station 3. Be sure to leave this sheet here.

STATION 3

As a group, read 1 Corinthians 13:6-7 and follow the instructions below.

1. Take turns answering this question:
   - Which of the characteristics in these verses seems to be most important in helping you love your family? Why?

2. Split into pairs (or trios). In your pairs, take turns interviewing each other, using the following questions. The interviewer needs to write down the answers.
   - Think of a person in your family who demonstrates one of these characteristics. Who are you thinking of, and what characteristic does that person demonstrate?
   - What does that person do to demonstrate that characteristic to the rest of the family?
   - What could you do to be more like that person?

3. Share with the rest of your family group some of the responses to the questions.

   At the leader's instruction, move to Station 1. Be sure to leave this sheet here.

Permission to photocopy this handout from Faith 4 Life: Junior High Bible Study Series, *My Family Life* granted for local church use. Copyright © Group Publishing, Inc., P.O. Box 481, Loveland, CO 80539. www.grouppublishing.com

Study 2

"My Teenagers Just Don't Understand Me!"

"It's not fair!"

"You don't understand!"

"Because I said so!"

Heard in homes all across the country, these battle cries may be familiar to the teenagers in your group. Put a teenager and a parent in a room together, and it probably won't be long before some form of disagreement arises.

So does this mean that all families with teenagers are by definition dysfunctional? Not at all! It just means that the process of raising a child—and of being raised—to adulthood can be pretty challenging at times.

This study helps teenagers take an honest look at the big picture of the parent-teenager relationship—what it's really like, how it got that way, and how to make it better. By acknowledging the sovereignty of God as their true Father, teenagers will be better equipped to see and understand the needs of their earthly parents.

The Study at a Glance

Warm-Up (10-15 minutes)

May I Help You?
What students will do: Act as parents as they serve their families.

Needs:
- ❏ newsprint
- ❏ markers
- ❏ paper plates
- ❏ tape
- ❏ scrap paper

What students will do: Discuss the typical parent-teenager relationship.

Needs:
- ❏ newsprint
- ❏ markers
- ❏ tape

Bible Connection (15-20 minutes)

Pulling Away
What students will do: Experience what it feels like to pull away from parents.

Needs:
- ❏ Bibles
- ❏ large rubber bands

Life Application (20-25 minutes)

Turning the Tables
What students will do: Discuss ways to show love and respect to parents, pray for their parents, and commit to showing them love.

Needs:
- ❏ Bibles
- ❏ paper
- ❏ pens or markers
- ❏ dictionaries
- ❏ masking tape
- ❏ paper wads from the "May I Help You?" activity
- ❏ "Getting to Know You" handouts (p. 24)

The Point

▶ As a Christian, you should treat your parents with respect and love.

Scripture Source

1 Corinthians 13:11-13; Ephesians 5:1-2
Paul urges us to show love.

Ephesians 6:1-3
Paul reminds us to follow the first commandment with a promise: to honor our parents in Christ.

Before the Study

If you choose to do the Bonus Activity, tape a sheet of newsprint to a classroom wall. Draw a vertical line to create two columns. Label one column, "What Parents Say" and the other column, "What Teenagers Say."

For the "Turning the Tables" activity at the end of the study, make the shape of a heart on the floor with masking tape. Make copies of the "Getting to Know You" handout (p. 24) for each student. You may want to give them multiple copies so students and their parents can answer the questions directly on the sheet.

Warm-Up

May I Help You?

(10 to 15 minutes)

Tape a piece of newsprint to the wall and

SAY:

- To see what it's like to be a parent, let's list some of the ways that parents serve us every day. Tell me some things that your parents have done for you in the last week or some things that you normally expect your parents to do for you.

Encourage teenagers to call out some of the responsibilities that parents have every day. Write teenagers' responses on the newsprint. Make the list of jobs as exhaustive as possible. You may want to help teenagers come up with ideas by asking specific questions, such as "Who usually pays the electric bill?" or "Who takes you to the doctor when you're sick?"

After you've written as many parental responsibilities as teenagers can come up with,

SAY:

- Parents are pretty busy people! Now let's look at our list and put a check mark next to each thing parents do for others, as opposed to what they do strictly for themselves.

After you've marked the answers,

ASK:

- Looking at our check marks, would you say that parents spend

> Be sensitive to teenagers who don't live with their parents or who have other legal guardians. If necessary, use the phrase "parents or guardians" to include any authority figure in your teenagers' lives.

more time doing things for themselves or for others? Explain.
- Do you think parents are servants? Why or why not?
- What does the word *servant* mean?
- How do you think your parents feel about serving?

SAY:

- Let's see how it might feel to be a parent.

Have teenagers form groups of four, and have groups gather at one end of the room. Give each group a pile of scrap paper, one marker, and a paper plate.

SAY:

- Choose one person in your group to be the parent. Decide if your parent is to be called Mom or Dad. The rest of you will be the family. The parent in your group will hold the paper plate up with one hand, like a waiter carrying a tray.

  When I say "go," the parent will attempt to walk to the opposite wall and back, holding the paper plate high in the air. The rest of you will each write on the paper scraps specific tasks you want your parent to do. For example, you might write, "Take me to the mall!" or "Make my dinner!"

  When you've written a task, wad up the paper scrap and call out, "Mom!" or "Dad!" to your parent. Your parent will then have to come back to the starting place. When you've called out what task you want your parent to do, place your paper wad on the plate. Then the parent can begin walking again until he or she is called back by someone else. We'll see if the parents are able to accomplish the goal of walking to the wall and back.

Play for a few minutes, then let teenagers switch roles. If you have time, give each teenager a chance to be the parent.

After the game, have teenagers sit with their families and discuss the following questions.

ASK:

- What was it like to be a family member in this game?
- What was it like to be the parent in this game?
- What kinds of emotions do you think parents experience as they try to get through a hectic day?

Refer teenagers back to the phrases you wrote on the newsprint in the first activity.

> This game is liable to get a little loud and frantic. That's OK since you're trying to give teenagers an idea of what a parent's fast-paced life is like.

ASK:

- After seeing what it might be like to be a parent, would you change any of the phrases listed? Why or why not?
- Why do you think it's sometimes hard to show respect and love to your parents?

SAY:

- Sometimes it's hard to remember that parents are people, too. They have worries and fears, just as you do. And just as in our game, they have lots of responsibilities. <u>As a Christian, you should treat your parents with respect and love.</u> But showing love and respect isn't always easy to do. Let's look at why that may be true.

◀ **The Point**

Save the paper wads to use later in the study.

Bonus Activity

(5 to 10 minutes)

If you'd like, begin your study with this additional activity.

After teenagers arrive,

SAY:

- Today we're going to talk about parents. But first we need to get an idea of what the typical parent-teenager relationship actually looks like. When I say "go," I want you to call out phrases that you think teenagers often say to or about their parents.

Encourage teenagers to call out phrases. On the newsprint you prepared before the study, write teenagers' responses in the column marked, "What Teenagers Say." Then

SAY:

- Now call out phrases that you think parents often say to or about their teenagers.

Record those answers in the "What Parents Say" column.

ASK:

- What do these phrases tell you about the typical parent-teenager relationship?
- Why do you think it's sometimes difficult for parents and teenagers to get along? Explain.

Have teenagers form pairs.

SAY:

- Discuss the following questions with your partner. After each question, each pair will have an opportunity to share its answers with the rest of the group.

ASK:
- What kinds of issues do you think parents and teenagers most often disagree about?
- What is the biggest source of disagreement between you and your parents?
- How do you usually resolve conflicts with your parents?

After pairs have had a chance to discuss the questions, encourage teenagers to share their answers with the whole group.

SAY:
- Sometimes it seems as though parents and teenagers come from two different worlds. And that's actually kind of true. Parents and teenagers have very different lives, and it may be hard for them to really understand each other. Parents might remember what it was like to be a teenager, even though times were different. But teenagers have no idea what it's like to be a parent because they haven't become parents yet.

    And because of that, it might be hard for you to realize that <u>your parents need you to treat them with respect and love</u>. Let's take a closer look at how parents really feel. ◄ **The Point**

Bible Connection: Pulling Away

(15 to 20 minutes)

SAY:
- I heard a story once about a mother who took her young teenage daughter to the doctor because of a sore throat. When the doctor walked into the examining room, the first thing he asked was, "How are you two getting along?" The mother and daughter, who seemed to be arguing more and more those days, looked at each other and rolled their eyes. "Not so great," the daughter answered. The doctor said, "Glad to hear it! I'd be worried if you *were* getting along." Seeing the puzzled look on their faces, he asked, "You know why you're fighting, don't you?"

    Instantly, the mother thought, "Yes, because she doesn't listen and is always crabby, and..." Meanwhile, the daughter was thinking, "Because she's always yelling at me, and she doesn't have a clue about my life, and..."

Then the doctor said, "You're fighting because you love each other, and it hurts to say goodbye. And that's what you're starting to say to each other—goodbye. You're beginning to pull away from each other. And if you didn't love each other, it wouldn't hurt."

ASK:

- What does it mean to be independent from your parents?
- At what age do you think teenagers start to pull away from their parents?

Let teenagers discuss the topic and agree on a specific age. Then have teenagers form pairs, and have pairs gather at one end of the room. Give each pair a large rubber band. Direct partners to stand side by side and join wrists, using the rubber bands. Then have pairs slowly walk to the other end of the room, counting off the steps as they go. Explain that each step represents one year of age.

As teenagers count steps and reach the agreed-upon age that teenagers start to pull away from their parents, have them begin to pull away from each other as they continue walking slowly. They'll still be joined by the rubber bands, but they'll feel tension on their wrists.

After each pair has gone through the pulling-away process, have teenagers discuss the following questions with their partners. After each question, give pairs the opportunity to share their insights with the rest of the group.

ASK:

- What happened when you began to pull away from your partner?
- How is that like pulling away from your parents?
- How do you know when you and your parents are pulling away from each other?

SAY:

- Sometimes pulling away from your parents can be painful, but that doesn't mean you no longer love each other. Thankfully, most parents and teenagers only pull away from each other for a time; they don't actually break away completely. As teenagers grow up to become adults, relationships with parents usually begin to come back together. But this pulling away brings up some interesting questions.

> If you have a large group or a small room, have pairs take turns walking across the room.

> Caution teenagers not to pull away from each other too hard or too quickly. Also, tell teenagers to stop pulling away if the rubber bands begin causing pain.

ASK:

- When you pull away from your parents, you know what you're pulling away *from*, but what are you pulling *toward*?
- Why are your parents pulling away from you?
- Why is it important to have a direction planned as you pull away from your parents?
- How can the Bible help you know what direction to head?

Distribute Bibles and have teenagers read 1 Corinthians 13:11-13 in their pairs. Then

ASK:

- According to this passage, what feeling should guide your actions?
- Why is it sometimes hard to show love to your parents?

SAY:

The Point ▶

- Pulling away from your parents can hurt—it can hurt you, and it can hurt your parents. But the Bible says that we should love one another, and that means loving parents, too! One way to do this is to remember that when you're feeling pain because of pulling away, your parents are feeling pain as well. That's why it's important to remember that your parents need your respect and love. They don't just *want* it. They don't just *deserve* it. They *need* it.

Let's concentrate now on how you can treat your parents with respect and love.

Life Application

Turning the Tables

(20 to 25 minutes)

Have teenagers form groups of four. You'll need the paper wads from the "May I Help You?" activity.

SAY:

- The Bible is clear about how parents and teenagers should act toward each other.

Give each group a sheet of paper, a pen or marker, a dictionary, and a Bible.

SAY:

■ I'm sure you're all familiar with the commandment that says to honor your father and mother. In fact, you may be so familiar with it that you may not have thought carefully about what it really means. Let's take a closer look.

Have teenagers in each group choose someone to be the reader and another person to be the recorder. Ask the reader in each group to read Ephesians 6:1-3 aloud. Then

SAY:

■ Look up the words *honor* and *obey* in the dictionary. Then have your recorder write down key words that define each term.

Give teenagers a few minutes to follow your instructions. Then have groups share their answers to the following questions:

■ What key words did you find to define *honor*?
■ What key words did you find to define *obey*?

Now evenly distribute among each group the paper wads and pens or markers from the earlier activity.

SAY:

■ In our earlier activity, we used these paper wads to record all the ways we expect our parents to serve us. Now let's look at some ways we can honor and obey our parents by serving them in the same situations.

Instruct teenagers to unfold each paper wad and brainstorm ideas about how they could serve their parents in the situations written on the papers. Have them write their answers on the unfolded paper. For example, if the paper wad reads, "Make my dinner," a teenager might write, "May I help you make dinner tonight?" Encourage them to refer to the key words they came up with for *honor* and *obey* if they get stumped.

Give teenagers time to go through all the paper wads and think of ways to honor their parents. Then

SAY:

■ <u>As a Christian, you can honor your parents by showing them the respect and love they need.</u> We saw in this activity that we can honor and serve our parents in as many ways as they serve us. And by honoring our parents, we'll please them and please God.   ◄ **The Point**

Have teenagers sit in a circle around the masking tape heart you prepared before the study. Place the unfolded papers in the center of the heart.

SAY:

- Today we've talked a lot about parents. You've learned that when you honor your parents, you're pleasing God. Pretty soon you may not need your parents in the way you do now. But you'll never outgrow your need for God. He's the perfect Father, and he'll always be there for you.

Choose a student to read aloud Ephesians 5:1-2 for the whole group. Then

SAY:

- Turn to a partner, and describe how it makes you feel to be a dearly loved child of God.

Give teenagers a few moments to share, then

SAY:

- The Bible says we should be imitators of God and live a life of love as his children. Look at all these papers in our circle—they're all ways to show our parents the respect and love they need. Because Jesus loves us, we can love others—including our parents!

  Choose a paper from inside the heart. As we go around the circle, say to the person on your left, "God loves you," and then quickly say one way that person can show love to his or her parents this week. I'll start.

Turn to the student on your left, and say something like, "God loves you, and you can show love to your parents by obeying them." Go around the circle until each student has had a chance to speak. Then

SAY:

- Let's take a moment now to silently thank God for our parents and to pray for them.

Close your time together in prayer. Encourage teenagers to pray a prayer of commitment, asking God to help them love and honor their parents.

Distribute copies of the "Getting to Know You" handout (p. 24) as students are leaving. Encourage them to take the quiz at home with their parents to discover just how much they really understand each other and to build understanding and mutual respect.

Getting to Know You

How well do you really understand your parents? Try this experiment to find out. Get together with your parent. Both of you should answer the questions for your parent. For instance, if you're talking with your dad, he should answer the questions as he normally would, but you should answer the way you truly believe he would answer them. Remember, answering like your mom or dad will show them you actually understand them better than they think you do.

When you've both answered the questions, go back over them and discuss your answers. How many of your answers match your parent's? Do any of your parent's answers surprise you? Why or why not? Try it with another parent, or switch and answer the questions for you to see how well your parent understands you.

The television family our family is most like is...

My favorite food is...

My favorite music is...

If I could go anywhere or do anything on vacation, I'd choose...

One thing I'm most proud of being good at is...

My favorite memory of our family is...

One of the happiest days of my life was...

What I like most about my life is...

One thing I'd change if I could is...

One of my dreams for the future is...

I really like it when my family...

It hurts my feelings when my family...

It makes me angry when...

What I'd like most from you is...

What makes me most proud of you is...

The best gift you ever gave me was...

The best gift I ever gave you was...

One thing I wish you knew about me is...

I'm so glad our family...

I wish our family...

Honoring Your Parents— No Matter What

Study 3

What would you do if your brother had raped your little sister—and your father chose to do nothing about it? Or what if your father ignored you for five years? How would you respond? How would you honor your father in a situation like that?

That was the life Absalom lived under his father, David. Absalom went on to lead a rebellion against his father, toward whom he no doubt felt resentment. We might criticize Absalom's choices now, but how many of us would have acted faultlessly if we had been in his shoes?

Honoring parents can be difficult, especially when they do things that hurt us. But God wants all of us to honor our parents regardless of what they do. Even though your students are young and their parents are certainly far from perfect, God expects children to honor their parents.

This study guides teenagers on an exploration of two brothers, Absalom and Solomon, and compares how well each son honored his parents— even when his parents didn't honor him in return.

Use this study to help teenagers discover practical ways to honor their parents—regardless of how their parents treat them.

The Point

▶ God wants you to honor your parents.

Scripture Source

Exodus 20:12
God commands his people to honor their parents.

**2 Samuel 13:1–18:18;
1 Kings 2:1–4:34**
Older brother Absalom rebels against his father, but younger brother Solomon honors and obeys.

Proverbs 6:20-23
Solomon offers advice on the importance of obeying parents.

The Study at a Glance

Warm-Up (5-10 minutes)

Honor Soup
What students will do: Use Scripture to help create an assortment of definitions of *honor* and then merge them into one.

Needs: ❑ Bibles ❑ tape
❑ newsprint ❑ markers
❑ paper ❑ pens

Bible Connection (25-30 minutes)

A Presentation of Honor
What students will do: Prepare and present two skits that illustrate how Absalom and Solomon treated their parents, and evaluate how well Absalom and Solomon honored their parents.

Needs: ❑ Bibles ❑ tape
❑ pens ❑ marker
❑ newsprint
❑ "Solomon" skit (p. 37)
❑ "Absalom" skit (p. 36)
❑ teenagers' definition of *honor* from "Honor Soup" activity

Bonus Activity (15-20 minutes)

What students will do: Interact with people older than they are about what they have learned about honoring, obeying, respecting, and getting along with parents.

Needs: ❑ older teenagers and adults for a panel discussion

Life Application (15-20 minutes)

My Personal Honor
What students will do: Evaluate how well they honored their parents in the past week, and commit to honoring their parents in specific ways in the coming week.

Needs: ❑ Bibles ❑ paper
❑ pens
❑ teenagers' definition of *honor* from "Honor Soup" activity

Before the Study

For "Honor Soup," tape a sheet of newsprint to a wall, and write "Honor" across the top. Then list these Bible references: Exodus 20:12; Proverbs 6:20-23.

For the "Presentation of Honor" activity, make two photocopies of the "Absalom" skit (p. 36) and two photocopies of the "Solomon" skit (p. 37).

If you choose to use the Bonus Activity, invite three to five guests to form a panel to discuss what they've learned about honoring, obeying, respecting, and getting along with parents. Invite one or two mature teenagers a few years older than your students. Invite adults of various ages, with an assortment of background experiences, who will relate well to teenagers and be good role models. Inform them in advance of your topic of discussion. You may want to give them a list of possible questions to get them thinking along the right lines.

For the "My Personal Honor" activity, create a sample timeline on a sheet of newsprint. Here's an example:

Sunday—Went to church with parents. Didn't talk about anything.

Monday—Mom made me dinner. I ate it in my room so I could play video games.

Tuesday—Talked to Mom a little in the morning.

Wednesday—Mom and Dad got mad at me about a grade on an English quiz.

Thursday—Nothing happened.

Friday—Parents went out to dinner. I stayed home and talked on phone.

Saturday—Mom and Dad made me do some work around the house. Left to go to a friend's house as soon as I had finished. Watched television with parents for a while on Saturday night.

Warm-Up

Honor Soup

(5 to 10 minutes)

Have teenagers form pairs, and direct their attention to the sheet of newsprint you posted on the wall before the study. Give each pair a Bible, a sheet of paper, and a pen.

SAY:

■ **Read the passages I've listed on the newsprint, then, based** on those passages, write a definition of the word *honor*. Start your definition by writing, "To honor people means to...," and then complete the sentence.

> **FYI**
>
> Some of your teenagers' parents may be divorced, absent, alcoholic, or addicted to drugs. A few of them may even be abusive. As you talk about the importance of honoring parents, be sensitive to teenagers who are in situations like these. Let teenagers know that you realize not every home is perfect and that honoring parents can be very challenging. Offer to talk privately with anyone who wants to. If a student talks about abuse taking place in his or her family, tell your pastor immediately. Remember that you may have a legal responsibility to report suspected abuse to official authorities.

After a couple of minutes, gather teenagers together. Have one pair write its definition on the newsprint. Then have a second pair add its definition to the first one. For example, if the first pair writes, "To honor people means to treat them with respect," the second pair could add, "never lie to them." Continue this process until each pair has added its definition.

You should end up with one long, detailed definition—for example, "To honor people means to treat them with respect, never lie to them, help them, obey them, listen to them, remember what they tell you, let them teach you, and don't think of yourself more highly than them."

Once the mega-definition is complete, allow teenagers to make any changes they want—editing questionable phrases or merging redundant ideas—until they come up with a detailed, biblical definition of *honor*.

When the mega-definition is finalized,

> If you have more than ten students, have teenagers form groups of six or fewer so each group can create its own "megadefinition" of honor. Then bring the whole class back together for the discussion.

ASK:

- Was it hard for you to merge your definition with all the others? Why or why not?
- How is merging our definitions together like this a way of honoring each other's perspectives?
- Would you like to be honored in the way this definition describes? Why or why not?
- Who should we honor in the way this definition describes? Why?
- Who do you have the most trouble honoring in the way this definition describes? Explain.

SAY:

- For a lot of us, it is not hardest to honor teachers or pastors or government leaders—it's hardest to honor our parents. That's because by now we've all learned that our parents are

> If your students come up with definition ideas for *honor* that don't correspond with the Bible, ask them to explain how they got their ideas from the passages you assigned.

The Point ▶

not perfect—and some might even be considered "bad." But today we're going to talk about why God wants you to honor your parents regardless of whether you think they're good or bad. We'll investigate how some young people in the Bible honored or didn't honor their parents, and we'll evaluate how well we honor our own parents, based on the definition you've just created.

Bible Connection

A Presentation of Honor
(25 to 30 minutes)

Have teenagers form two groups. Give one group two copies of the "Absalom" skit (p. 36), and give the other group two copies of the "Solomon" skit (p. 37). Assign teenagers the various roles, or let students choose the roles for themselves. If you have more students than parts, extra students may act as the optional players listed in the skits.

> If you have more than twenty-five students, have teenagers form four groups instead of two; then have each group perform its own version of either the "Absalom" or "Solomon" skit.
>
> If you have fewer than fifteen students, have teenagers play multiple parts in the skits. To help teenagers separate their characters, give them props to use with each character. For example, a broomstick "spear" could be a prop for Absalom, while a hat could be a "crown" for King David. Have teenagers switch props, depending on which character they're portraying.

After all the parts are assigned, have groups read their assigned skits to familiarize themselves with the stories. Then

SAY:

■ We're going to do these skits as impromptu performances. Just act out whatever the narrators say, and ham it up as much as you like. As the skits are presented, think about how well Absalom and Solomon measured up to our definition of *honor* in the way they treated their parents. Through these examples, we want to find out why God wants you to honor your parents.

The Point ▶

Have groups take turns presenting their skits to the rest of the class. Applaud students' efforts, and congratulate them on their spontaneous creativity. Then have teenagers form groups of four to discuss these questions:

- What's your reaction to the story of Absalom? of Solomon?
- Do you think Absalom got what he deserved? Why or why not?
- Did Solomon get what he deserved? Why or why not?
- Would you consider King David a good father? Explain.
- If you were David, what would you have done differently as a father?
- What would you have done differently if you were Absalom? Solomon?
- What do these stories teach us about honoring our parents?

SAY:

- God wants you to honor your parents. And stories like the ones we just heard are included in the Bible so we can learn what honoring our parents really means. Now that we know something about the family life of these two brothers, let's take a closer look at how they did—or did not—honor their parents through their choices.

◀ **The Point**

Have teenagers stay in their groups; give each group paper, pens, and a Bible. Point to the definition of *honor* that teenagers created in the first activity, and

SAY:

- This is the measuring rod we've decided to use to determine whether these brothers honored their parents. Think about the skit you presented and the skit you watched, then take a few minutes to look through the stories in Scripture—2 Samuel 13:1–18:18 and 1 Kings 2:1–4:34.

Give teenagers a few minutes to scan through the Scripture passages, then

SAY:

- Using this definition, rate how well each brother honored his parents. On your paper, write two scores—one for Absalom and one for Solomon. You may want to look up parts of the stories to help you decide. Use a rating scale from 1 to 10, with 10 being absolute perfection and 1 being utter failure. For example, if you think one brother did most things right but messed up in a few areas, you might rate him at 7 or 8. But, hey, you're the judge. You make the call. We'll talk about your scores in a few minutes.

Tell teenagers that everyone must offer a score for both Absalom and Solomon. Explain that to come up with a final score for each brother, each group should average its group members' scores. For example, if one group's members rate Absalom at 3, 5, 5, and 6, the average is almost 5 (4.75).

To help groups decide how to rate each brother, encourage them to think about what each brother did (did his actions honor his parents?); what motivated each brother's actions (did he *try* to honor his parents, even if it didn't work out the way he wanted?); and what other people said or wrote about each brother's actions (did other people think he honored his parents?).

While groups decide their scores, tape a sheet of newsprint to a wall. At the top, write, "Honor Score." Then draw a line down the center of the newsprint. On one side, write "Absalom"; on the other side, write "Solomon."

When groups are ready, have them present their scores. Write each group's scores on the newsprint. Then

ASK:
- Why did you rate Absalom the way you did?
- According to our definition of *honor*, what do you think Absalom should have done differently to honor his parents?
- Why did you rate Solomon the way you did?
- According to our definition, what do you think Solomon should have done differently to honor his parents?
- How might the skit have been different if Absalom or Solomon had honored his parents in the way you suggest?
- Why should Absalom and Solomon have cared whether they honored their parents?

The Point ▶
- Why do you think God wants you to honor your parents?

Bonus Activity

(15 to 20 minutes)

If you'd like, include this additional activity in your study.

Start this activity by inviting your guests to the front of the room to form a panel for discussion. As you ask the following questions, allow guests to speak and build on what others on the panel have said, until students feel comfortable enough to keep things going with their own questions and comments.

SAY:

- **We're pleased to have some guests with us to talk about parents today.** (Introduce your guests by name, and tell briefly their qualifications for being on this panel.) **I'm going to start by asking our guests some questions. Listen carefully to what they say, and feel free to raise your hand and ask questions or make comments.**

ASK:

- What was your relationship with your parents like when you were twelve or thirteen?
- What is your relationship with your parents like now?
- What was the hardest time for you to get along with your parents?
- Over the years, what have you learned about honoring, loving, obeying, and respecting parents?
- How has the way you view your parents changed over the years?
- How did you handle it when your parents disappointed you?
- What advice would you give these teenagers so they don't have to make mistakes you might have made in your relationship with your parents?
- What can teenagers do to improve their relationship with their parents?
- Is a parent's mistake or failure ever an excuse for not honoring and respecting him or her? Explain.
- How do you honor your parents?
- For those of you who are parents, what can your children do to let you know they honor and respect you?
- How does it feel when your children honor you? When they don't?

Conclude by asking students to discuss and synthesize the insights they gleaned from the guest speakers. Lead them in a prayer of commitment to honor, respect, and obey their parents.

Life Application

My Personal Honor
(15 to 20 minutes)

SAY:

The Point ▶

■ Evaluating how well Absalom and Solomon honored their parents is helpful. But the Bible teaches that <u>God wants you to honor your parents</u> too. So now let's make it personal.

Have each person find a partner from a different group. Distribute paper and pens, and have pairs discuss these questions:

■ What would you have said to Absalom if he had asked you for advice before doing anything the skit described?
■ What would you have said to Solomon?
■ Which brother is most like you? Explain.
■ Do you think it's important for you to honor your parents? Why or why not?
■ What makes it hard for you to honor your parents?

SAY:

■ On your paper, create a timeline of any interaction you've had with your parents in the past week. For example, make a note of every time you ate together, did something else together, or talked about anything. When you're finished, explain your timeline to your partner.

> To help teenagers create their timelines, display the sample timeline you prepared before the study.

Give students a few minutes to create their timelines. When teenagers have finished explaining their timelines to their partners, point to the definition of *honor* and

SAY:

■ Now it gets tough. Using this definition, rate yourself according to how well you honored your parents during the past week. Use the same approach you used with Absalom and Solomon. Write your personal score on the back of your timeline.

When teenagers finish, have them share their scores with their partners. Then have pairs discuss these questions:

■ How do you feel about your score? Explain.
■ Why did you rate yourself the way you did?

Invite a volunteer to read aloud Proverbs 6:20-23, then

ASK:

- Do you think Solomon's advice in this passage is true for your family? Why or why not?
- What makes it hard for you to honor your parents in the way our definition describes?
- What advice can you offer yourself on how you can improve your score?
- What advice can you offer your partner on how to improve his or her score?

After the discussion,

SAY:

- <u>God wants you to honor your parents</u>, but it won't always be easy. By praying for God's strength and wisdom, we can learn to honor our parents in ways that please God—even when our parents aren't perfect. ◀ **The Point**

Have teenagers stay in pairs. Based on the definition of *honor* and all they've discussed, have teenagers each think of two practical things they can do in the coming week to honor their parents. For example, teenagers might decide to ask their parents about their day, offer to help clean the kitchen, or do their homework without being asked. Have teenagers write their ideas underneath their personal scores and share what they wrote with their partners. Then have partners pray together, asking God to give them the strength and wisdom to honor their parents.

When the prayer time is concluded,

> To help teenagers come up with practical ideas for honoring their parents, photocopy the "Ten Great Ways for Teenagers to Honor Their Parents" **FYI** (p. 35), and give each person a copy.

SAY:

- <u>God wants you to honor your parents</u>, and we can help each other accomplish that goal. On your own sheet, copy the two ideas your partner came up with. Commit to pray for your partner at least once this week, asking God to help your partner honor his or her parents this week. Then, sometime next week, ask your partner how the week went. You'll be surprised at how much things can change with just a little effort. ◀ **The Point**

Direct teenagers one more time to their definition of *honor*.

SAY:

- For our closing, look over this definition and tell your partner one aspect of this definition you already see in his or her life. For example, you might say, "You're always honest" or "You're a good listener."

When pairs have finished, dismiss the class. Encourage them to take home their timelines as reminders to honor their parents in the coming week.

Ten Great Ways for Teenagers to Honor Their Parents

1. Say "thank you" often.
2. Tell them how your day went—using more than five words.
3. Clean up the kitchen, take out the trash, mow the lawn, or do other household chores—without being asked.
4. Be nice to your siblings.
5. Ask permission before inviting friends over or going somewhere with friends.
6. Ask your parents for advice—even if it's about little things such as which toothpaste you should use.
7. When you do something wrong, admit it and ask for forgiveness.
8. Speak highly of them when they're not around.
9. Say "I love you" often.
10. When you don't know what else to do, hug them.

Some of your students may be victims of parents who abuse them verbally, physically, or sexually. Abuse in any form is a serious problem and should not be taken lightly. If students make comments during the study that cause you to suspect abuse, talk to them privately about their situations at home. Don't pressure students for information, and don't ask leading questions. Just listen closely to what your students say to make sure you understand what they're telling you. For example, a student who says he feels "beat up" at home may not mean to imply that his parents beat him. He may just be using a figure of speech.

After talking with students, if you believe abuse may be occurring, immediately notify your pastor. Remember that you may have a legal responsibility to report suspected abuse to official authorities. Your church most likely has information on local counseling agencies that can help abusive families change their behavior.

Absalom

Players: Absalom (son of King David), Tamar (Absalom's sister), Amnon (Absalom's half-brother), King David (the parent), Joab (David's military leader), Narrator 1, Narrator 2

Optional players: Fighting men, a large oak tree, horses (for whoever pursues or is pursued), a mule, three javelins, the people

Narrator 1: This is the story of Absalom (pronounced *AB-sah-lum*) and King David that is based on 2 Samuel 13:1-18:18. Absalom was very close to his sister Tamar (*TAY-mahr*). They liked hanging out together and shooting the breeze. But they had a half brother, Amnon (*AM-non*), who was a real social deviant. He assaulted his sister Tamar. She was so hurt by what he did that she wanted to die. When Tamar told Absalom what Amnon had done, Absalom was furious. King David also heard about what happened, and he was angry too. But King David never did anything about the situation. He just turned a blind eye to the whole thing.

Narrator 2: Absalom, however, did do something. After plotting and scheming for two years, he came up with a plan. He threw a huge party and invited all the king's sons, including Amnon. At the party, Amnon was having a good time and drinking a lot of wine. After he got really drunk, Absalom had his men kill Amnon to avenge what Amnon had done to his sister Tamar.

Narrator 1: When King David heard about Amnon's murder, he became angry again. Absalom was scared about what the king might do, so he ran away and hid. Once again, though, King David did nothing about the situation. He didn't try to talk to Absalom or ask him to come back home; he didn't even punish him. The king just sat and moped around the palace. So Absalom stayed away for three years. And even though King David longed to see Absalom, he did nothing.

Narrator 2: King David's military leader, Joab (*JO-ab*), got really tired of David's moping around all the time. Finally, Joab helped David to realize that Absalom should come home, and David sent Joab to bring Absalom home. When Absalom returned to the city, though, the king refused to see him. David told Joab to tell Absalom that he was not allowed to come to the palace or see the king for any reason. So Absalom was really upset.

Narrator 1: After two years, Absalom couldn't take it anymore. He told his men to set Joab's fields on fire to get Joab's attention. When Joab asked Absalom about the fire, Absalom demanded to see his father. King David gave in and agreed to see Absalom. When they met, they hugged and made up—or so it seemed. But really, Absalom was still very angry about what his father had done. So Absalom plotted a rebellion against the king.

Narrator 2: Absalom began telling the people, "If I were king, things would be different. I would be a better king than my father, David." After years of this, Absalom asked his men to fight with him to overthrow the king. The men agreed. When the king heard about the rebellion, he and almost everyone at the palace ran away. So Absalom declared himself king in his father's place.

Narrator 1: King David gathered his own men and asked them to fight Absalom's men. But David told his men not to harm Absalom, even though he had overthrown David's kingdom. Joab led David's fighting men out to find Absalom's army. By chance, one of David's men saw Absalom. Absalom had been riding a mule under a large oak tree, and his long hair had gotten tangled in the branches. The branches had pulled Absalom off his donkey and had left him dangling in the tree. David's fighting men refused to kill Absalom because of the king's order. But when Joab saw Absalom, he speared three javelins through Absalom's heart.

Narrator 2: Then David's men took Absalom out of the tree and buried him in the forest under a pile of rocks.

Permission to photocopy this handout from Faith 4 Life: Junior High Bible Study Series, *My Family Life* granted for local church use. Copyright © Group Publishing, Inc., P.O. Box 481, Loveland, CO 80539. www.grouppublishing.com

Solomon

Players: Solomon (son of King David), Benaiah (Solomon's military leader), Joab (David's military leader), Shimei (an enemy of King David's), King David (the parent), God, Narrator 1, Narrator 2

Optional players: Fighting men, the altar, two slaves, a donkey

Narrator 1: This is a story of Solomon and David that is based on 1 Kings 2:1–4:34. Solomon was not King David's oldest son, but David had decided to make Solomon king after him anyway. So when King David was on his deathbed, he called Solomon to him to give a few last-minute instructions.

Narrator 2: King David asked Solomon to clear up some of David's unfinished business. For example, David asked Solomon to have Joab (pronounced *JO-ab*) killed because Joab had killed people he shouldn't have killed. David also asked Solomon to keep an eye on a fellow named Shimei (*SHIM-ee-i*). That's because Shimei had sided with Absalom (*AB-sah-lum*) during the rebellion and had actually thrown rocks at David as he fled Jerusalem. After David had said these things, he died.

Narrator 1: As king, Solomon started to fulfill his father's requests. When Joab heard that King Solomon might be out to get him, he ran to the tent of the Lord and took hold of the altar, clinging to it like a baby to his mother. Solomon heard that Joab was there, so he sent Benaiah (*bee-NAY-uh*) to kill him. Benaiah tried to get Joab to come away from the altar, but he refused. After consulting with King Solomon again, Benaiah killed him anyway—right there by the altar.

Narrator 2: Next King Solomon summoned Shimei and said to him, "I've decided not to kill you for what you did to my father. But I command you to stay in Jerusalem, where I can keep an eye on you for as long as you live. The day you leave Jerusalem will be the day you die." Shimei agreed to the king's terms and stayed in Jerusalem for three years. But then…

Narrator 1: Two of Shimei's slaves escaped, so Shimei saddled his donkey and went to fetch them. By the time he had returned to Jerusalem, King Solomon had heard that Shimei had left town. So the king called Shimei before him and asked, "Why did you not keep your oath to the Lord and obey me?" Then Solomon asked Benaiah to kill Shimei. And Benaiah did.

Narrator 2: After Solomon had fulfilled his father's requests, the Lord appeared to Solomon in a dream. God told Solomon to ask for whatever he wanted God to give to him. Solomon said, "You have been faithful to my father, David, because he was righteous and upright in heart. Now you've made me king in his place. But I am too young to know how to rule well. So give me wisdom and discernment so I can govern your people well."

Narrator 1: God was really pleased with Solomon's request, so he said, "Because you asked for this instead of wealth, long life, or victory over your enemies, I will not only grant your request, but I will also give you all the things you didn't ask for. I will give you riches and honor above all other kings during your lifetime. And if you obey me as your father did, I will give you a long life."

Narrator 2: Solomon became the wisest man who ever lived. He spoke three thousand proverbs; wrote more than one thousand songs; and studied plant life, animals, birds, reptiles, and fish. People came from all around to benefit from Solomon's wisdom.

Study 4

Why Can't We Just Get Along?

It's a problem the very first family faced: Siblings have a tough time getting along.

You don't have to get very far into the Bible to find siblings who definitely were *not* the best of friends. Even when sibling rivalry was not expressed violently (as it was in the story of Cain and Abel in Genesis 4), it certainly caused discord.

Unfortunately, not a lot has changed. Teenagers still struggle with their siblings.

Much the way brothers and sisters in the Bible treated each other, siblings today often take each other for granted, fail to be considerate, and look to place blame. When talking about their siblings, teenagers frequently complain about such issues as dishonesty during play, name-calling, disregard for privacy and personal property, and competition for attention.

SIBLINGS

DIVISION

In contrast to the behavior just described, the Bible encourages us to "keep on loving each other as brothers" (Hebrews 13:1), implying that love between siblings should be the model for love between people in general and believers in particular.

But do your teenagers understand what that kind of love looks like?

In this study, teenagers will experience empathy, negotiation, teamwork, and appreciation. They'll discover that empathizing leads to negotiation, which fosters teamwork, which generates a feeling of appreciation for others. Through these experiences, teenagers will learn about brotherly love and will realize that despite differences, brothers and sisters can be friends.

The Study at a Glance

Warm-Up (10-15 minutes)

Best (Dressed) Foot Forward
What students will do: Learn about empathy by participating in a relay race wearing unusual footwear.

Needs:
- Bibles
- marker
- suitcase or bag
- small bag or box
- footwear as described in the "Before the Study" box (p. 40)
- masking tape
- clean socks
- paper scraps

Bonus Activity (10-15 minutes)
What students will do: Use teamwork to mentally and physically meet a challenge.

Needs:
- 2 rolls of crepe paper
- 2 rolls of tape

Bible Connection (25-30 minutes)

Sibling Scenarios
What students will do: Create presentations depicting conflicts between siblings, see the conflicts from each sibling's viewpoint, and practice negotiating solutions.

Needs:
- Bibles
- newsprint
- tape
- scissors
- marker
- "Sibling Scenarios" handouts (p. 46)

Life Application (10-15 minutes)

Finding Friends
What students will do: Acknowledge traits in one another that are desirable in friends and realize that siblings often have these same traits.

Needs:
- tape
- marker
- pens
- transparent tape
- newsprint
- colored paper
- scissors

The Point

▶ Through God's love, your brothers and sisters can be your friends.

Scripture Source

Genesis 37:17-28; Numbers 12:1-9; Luke 10:38-42
Conflict arises between brothers and sisters.

Matthew 5:23-24; 18:15, 21-22; Ephesians 4:1-3; 1 Peter 3:8-9; 1 John 4:19-21
Our conduct toward others should be loving.

Matthew 12:46-50
Jesus compares his followers to brothers and sisters.

Hebrews 13:1
We're to treat each other as brothers.

Before the Study

For the "Best (Dressed) Foot Forward" activity, gather several different pieces of footwear, such as a tennis shoe, a ballet slipper, a beach flipper, a clog, a rubber boot, and an old dress shoe. (Be sure you have an equal number of right shoes and left shoes.) On the bottom of each shoe, affix a piece of masking tape with a number written on it. For example, label the tennis shoe with a "1," the ballet slipper with a "2," and so on. Put the shoes, along with some clean socks, into a suitcase or bag. You'll also need to write the same numbers on scraps of paper and put the scraps in a small bag or box.

For the "Sibling Scenarios" activity, photocopy the "Sibling Scenarios" handout (p. 46), and cut the handout into separate scenarios. You'll also need to write the following Scripture references on a piece of newsprint and tape the newsprint to a wall: Matthew 5:23-24; Matthew 18:15; Matthew 18:21-22; Ephesians 4:1-3; 1 Peter 3:8-9; 1 John 4:19-21.

For the "Finding Friends" activity, cut colorful paper into 1-inch wide strips. Make sure you have one bracelet strip for each person, plus extra copies for students to make one for each brother and sister they have.

> The number of shoes you'll need depends on how many teams you'll use during the "Best (Dressed) Foot Forward" activity. You'll need only two shoes for each team, so if you have fewer than fifteen teenagers in your group, you'll need four shoes.

Warm-Up

Best (Dressed) Foot Forward

(10 to 15 minutes)

After everyone has arrived,

ASK:
- How many of you have brothers or sisters?
- What do you like about having brothers and sisters?
- What do you dislike about having brothers and sisters?

SAY:
- Most of us struggle to some degree with our siblings. But we can learn a lot about how to treat other people through our relationships with our brothers and sisters.

Ask volunteers to read aloud Matthew 12:46-50 and Hebrews 13:1.

> Throughout the study, remind teenagers who don't have brothers or sisters at home that they can learn from the study how to treat their brothers and sisters in Christ.

> You may want to allow team members to swap numbers so that each team has a right shoe and a left shoe.

ASK:
- Who do these Scriptures say our brothers and sisters are?
- Why do you think we're to treat each other "as brothers"?
- If the Bible says we're to treat each other as brothers, and if Jesus called believers his brothers and sisters, how do you think God feels about the relationship between siblings?

SAY:
- We may have brothers and sisters at home. Or we may have brothers and sisters in Christ. Regardless, we need to treat all our brothers and sisters the way God wants us to. So today we're going to learn about some tools to help us get along with our siblings. Let's find out how, **through God's love, your brothers and sisters can be your friends.**

The Point ▶

Have teenagers form two teams and line up single file with their teammates at one end of the room. Put the suitcase of shoes and socks between the teams. Then have the first two people from each team choose two numbers from the small bag. Have those students find the corresponding shoes in the suitcase and then return to their teams.

Explain to teenagers that they will be participating in a relay in which they have to put on their teams' shoes, *walk*—not run—to the other end of the room and back, and then hand the shoes to the next person in line. Tell teenagers that the relay will continue until everyone has had a chance to walk across the room and back.

Allow teenagers to borrow a pair of socks from the suitcase, give them time to put the socks on, and then begin the relay. After the relay,

> If you have more than fourteen students, you may want to have teenagers form additional teams. Just be sure to provide two shoes for each team.

ASK:
- Was it easy or difficult to walk in someone else's shoes? Why?
- What does it mean to "walk a mile in someone else's shoes"?
- Is it usually easy or difficult to see a situation from someone else's viewpoint? Why?
- When dealing with your brothers and sisters, do you usually see situations from their viewpoints? Explain.
- How do you think your relationships with your siblings would be affected if you tried to see things from their viewpoints?

SAY:
- Even though you might not get along with your siblings all the time, your brothers and sisters can be your friends—especially if you learn to see things from your siblings' viewpoints. Let's look at some specific situations to see how that can work.

Bonus Activity

(10 to 15 minutes)

Try this Bonus Activity after "Best (Dressed) Foot Forward."

Have teenagers help you clear furniture from one area of the room. Divide the class into two groups, and have students stand in lines with their groups.

SAY:

- Imagine that your group is a caterpillar. I'm going to give the first person in each line a roll of crepe paper and a roll of tape, and each group has to figure out how to spin itself into a cocoon. There are only two rules. First, except for the lead person in each group, you must keep at least one hand on the shoulder of the person in front of you at all times. Second, you may not watch the other group.

Hand each lead person a roll of crepe paper and a roll of tape, and have groups begin.

After this activity, have teenagers "emerge" from their cocoons, then

ASK:

- What was it like to be connected to each other during this activity?
- What was easy or difficult about completing the task while you were all connected?
- How did working with others affect your caterpillar?
- Describe an occasion when you and a sibling had fun together even though you were "working" on something.
- How could you apply what you learned in accomplishing this challenge to working together with your brothers and sisters?

SAY:

- So far you've learned that when you try to see things from your siblings' viewpoints, you can negotiate good solutions to problems. And when you negotiate good solutions, you find that your brothers and sisters actually make good teammates. All that helps you to realize that, <u>through God's love, your brothers and sisters can be your friends</u>.

The Point ▶

> Teenagers might come up with many different ways to solve this "puzzle." For example, if the lead person tapes one end of the crepe paper to a chair and starts stretching the paper around the perimeter of a group of chairs (with the rest of his or her teammates following), the caterpillar can curl around inside the cocoon. Or a group might form a big circle and pass the roll of crepe paper from person to person (on the outside) so that it winds around the caterpillar.

Bible Connection

Sibling Scenarios

(25 to 30 minutes)

Have teenagers form six groups, and give each group a different scenario from the "Sibling Scenarios" handout (p. 46). Explain that groups will have a few minutes to read their scenarios and create a presentation.

SAY:

- In your presentations, you'll first need to summarize the conflict between the siblings in your scenario. You'll then need to present each sibling's viewpoint. Your group can be as creative as it wants to be to present this material, but everyone has to participate.

Give students about five minutes to prepare, then have each group take a turn presenting its scenario. Lead teenagers in applauding each group's efforts. After all the groups have presented,

ASK:

- What problems were the siblings in these scenarios facing?
- When you heard the different viewpoints, did your feelings or opinions about the conflict change? Why or why not?
- If the people in these scenarios could see things from their siblings' viewpoints, do you think they could work out their problems? Why or why not?

SAY:

- Each of us has felt jealousy or resentment toward others. Although it's natural to feel anger toward our siblings from time to time, the Bible tells us how we should treat our brothers and sisters.

From the newsprint you prepared before the study, assign each group one Scripture.

SAY:

- Your group will have another few minutes to read your Scriptures and create a new presentation. This time, you'll first need to summarize in your own words what the Scriptures tell us about how we should treat each other. You'll then need to present how the siblings in your scenario could negotiate a solution to their conflict if they considered each other's

---

For this activity, each group should have between two and six participants. Duplicate or subtract scenarios as needed to accommodate the number of teenagers in your group.

viewpoints and the principles from the Scriptures. Again, your group can be as creative as it wants to be in presenting this material. Just make sure everyone participates.

Give students about five minutes to prepare, then have each group take a turn presenting its solutions. Lead teenagers in applauding each group's efforts. After all the groups have presented,

ASK:

- From these presentations, what did you learn about how we should treat our brothers and sisters?
- What did you have to do to negotiate solutions?
- When the siblings considered each other's viewpoints as well as the principles in the Scriptures, how well were they able to negotiate solutions? Explain.
- If you used these guidelines with your brothers and sisters, what difference would it make? Explain.
- Why is it sometimes difficult to follow these guidelines?
- What do you think you should do if your siblings don't treat you according to these guidelines? Why?

SAY:

- It's important to understand that you can disagree with people and still love them. If we focus on Christ, though, we can be at peace with one another. And when we try to see things from someone else's viewpoint, we're better able to negotiate good solutions to problems. When we're willing to negotiate, we're one step closer to realizing that <u>through God's love, our brothers and sisters can be our friends</u>. Now let's practice the next step.

◀ **The Point**

Finding Friends

(10 to 15 minutes)

Tape a sheet of newsprint to a wall, and ask teenagers to call out qualities they look for or appreciate in friends. List their answers on the newsprint.

Have teenagers form pairs, and give everyone a pen and a bracelet strip. Have students write "Brothers and sisters can be friends" on their bracelets. Then ask each student to write on his or her bracelet a quality of a good friend that also describes his or her partner. Have teenagers exchange bracelets. Pass around tape for students to use to fasten their bracelets.

SAY:

- **If any of you has a brother or sister at home, raise your hand and keep it raised. If any of you has a brother or sister "in Christ," raise your hand also.**

  Take a look around the room at all of us who are siblings. Each of us has qualities that people look for in friends.

Have teenagers look at the newsprint list of qualities they look for or appreciate in friends.

ASK:

- **Which of these qualities do your brothers and sisters have?**
- **What qualities do your brothers and sisters have that *you* look for in friends?**

SAY:

- **Today we've talked about learning to see our siblings' viewpoints, negotiating with them, practicing teamwork, and appreciating their good qualities. This week, remember that through God's love, your brothers and sisters can be your friends, and try to use what you've learned today to be good friends to them.** ◄ **The Point**

Give students enough copies of the friendship bracelet so they can make one for each brother and sister they have. (Students who don't have brothers or sisters can make bracelets for brothers and sisters in the Lord.) Instruct them to write on each bracelet one specific way in which they see that sister or brother as a friend. For instance, "You look out for me when anyone tries to pick on me," "It's fun just hanging out with you," or "I'm glad we like the same music."

Encourage pairs to brainstorm one or two practical ideas for nurturing friendship with each sibling in the coming week. They might plan an outing together, focus on making conversation and giving compliments, look for opportunities to help them, and so on. They should write these down and each take a list home with them as a reminder.

Then have partners pray for each other—mentioning their partner's brothers and sisters by name—asking God to help them appreciate, love, get along with, and share true friendship with their brothers and sisters.

To close, lead students in a time of prayer for their siblings or other family members.

> While specific instructions regarding sibling relationships seem difficult to find in the Bible, many passages suggest that God wants families to provide centers of love and support from which members "fan out" to do his work. The first two words of the Lord's Prayer in Matthew 6:9, "Our Father," and passages such as Matthew 12:46-50; Galatians 3:26-28; and Ephesians 4:4-6 tell us that Christians are all brothers and sisters in a figurative sense.
>
> Although squabbles between siblings seem to be a fact of family life, brothers and sisters can be friends when empathy, negotiation, teamwork, and appreciation are encouraged.

Sibling Scenarios

Scenario 1
Genesis 37:17-28

When Joseph was a boy, he was his father's favorite son. Joseph's brothers were so jealous of him that they sold him as a slave to some slave traders. He ended up living as a house slave in Egypt.

Many years later, Joseph found himself in a position to either destroy or save his brothers. Because of a famine, Joseph's brothers went to Egypt to buy food. Joseph was then a governor of Egypt and had the power to either save his brothers or turn them away.

• Summarize the conflict between Joseph and his brothers.

• Present both Joseph's and the brothers' viewpoints as if they were explaining to someone how they felt and why they acted the way they did.

Scenario 2
Numbers 12:1-9

Miriam and Aaron were jealous of their brother Moses because he was God's spokesperson to the entire nation of Israel. They dealt with their feelings by complaining about Moses' wife, who was a foreigner.

God was not pleased with their behavior, and he gathered Moses, Miriam, and Aaron together to reprimand Miriam and Aaron. When God had finished talking, Miriam was suddenly sick with leprosy.

• Summarize the conflict between Miriam, Aaron, and Moses.

• Present Miriam's, Aaron's, and Moses' viewpoints as if they were explaining to someone how they felt and why they acted the way they did.

Scenario 3
Luke 10:38-42

Jesus taught in the home of two sisters, Mary and Martha. Mary sat, listening to Jesus, while Martha cleaned the home and prepared a meal. Exasperated, Martha complained to Jesus that Mary wasn't helping her and asked Jesus to chastise Mary.

• Summarize the conflict between Mary and Martha.

• Present both Mary's and Martha's viewpoints as if they were explaining to someone how they felt and why they acted the way they did.

Scenario 4

Bill was building a model airplane when Diane walked into the room. Although the television was on, Bill didn't appear to be watching it, so Diane changed the channel. Bill got mad, and they started arguing about who should be able to watch what.

• Summarize the conflict between Bill and Diane.

• Present both Bill's and Diane's viewpoints as if they were explaining to someone how they felt and why they acted the way they did.

Scenario 5

Jennifer's youth group was going bowling one evening, and she couldn't decide what to wear. She decided to borrow Tracy's blouse—without asking. Several hours later, Tracy frantically searched for her blouse while getting ready to go out with friends. She ended up putting on another outfit she didn't like nearly as much; then she saw Jennifer heading out the door in her blouse. They began to argue.

• Summarize the conflict between Jennifer and Tracy.

• Present both Jennifer's and Tracy's viewpoints as if they were explaining to someone how they felt and why they acted the way they did.

Scenario 6

Kevin and Jed are responsible for chores around the house, such as cleaning the kitty-litter box and mowing the yard. On Tuesday night, their mom asked whether the trash had been taken outside for collection the next morning. Kevin and Jed couldn't agree on whose turn it was to take out the trash.

• Summarize the conflict between Kevin and Jed.

• Present both Kevin's and Jed's viewpoints as if they were explaining to someone how they felt and why they acted the way they did.

Permission to photocopy this handout from Faith 4 Life: Junior High Bible Study Series, *My Family Life* granted for local church use.
Copyright © Group Publishing, Inc., P.O. Box 481, Loveland, CO 80539. www.grouppublishing.com

Changed 4 Life

My Family Life

To help students take what they've learned into their daily lives after they've finished this study, suggest at least one way each week that students can honor their families. You could make up a calendar marked with suggestions for each week and distribute it to students or send a weekly challenge in the mail or via e-mail. Tailor your challenges to your students' situations. Here are some suggestions for family challenges:

- Show respect for your parents by spending more time with them. Perhaps you could give up a trip to the mall or a school function to be with your parents.
- Initiate conversations with the members of your family. Make it easy for your family to talk to you.
- Pray daily for your family.
- Do something special for each member of your family.
- Talk with your parents about your day. Ask them about theirs and really listen.
- For each member of your family, do one chore or task that is typically their responsibility.
- Look for reasons to say, "Thank you." Say it sincerely. Say it a lot.
- Let your brother or sister pick what television program or movie you'll watch.
- Make breakfast for your family.
- Remember, even little acts of consideration, such as telling parents when your plans change or compromising with siblings, can make a big difference.

It's sometimes difficult for parents and teenagers to reach out to each other. Consider planning one of the following intergenerational activities to help the process along. If teenagers in your group aren't living with their parents, or have lost one or both parents, adapt these suggestions to include substitute caretakers or guardians.

- Plan a service project that teenagers and their families can do together. You could go as a group to clean up a local river or serve in a homeless shelter. Have families work on elements of the service project at home—making phone calls or gathering supplies, for example. Ensure opportunity for follow-up with an appreciation party after the service project has been accomplished.
- Have teenagers plan an event for their families. It could be a party, Bible study, or group outing. Offer limited help as teenagers work through the details on their own. That way they'll be more proud of the result.

Look for the Whole Family of Faith 4 LiFE Bible Studies!

Senior High Books
- Applying God's Word
- Believing in Jesus
- Christian Character
- Family Matters
- Following Jesus
- Is There Life After High School?
- Prayer
- Sexuality
- Sharing Your Faith
- Worshipping 24/7
- Your Christian ID
- Your Relationships

Junior High Books
- Becoming a Christian
- Choosing Wisely
- Fighting Temptation
- Finding Your Identity
- Friends
- God's Purpose for Me
- How to Pray
- My Family Life
- My Life as a Christian
- Sharing Jesus
- Understanding the Bible
- Who Is God?

Preteen Books
- Being Responsible
- Building Friendships
- Getting Along With Others
- God in My Life
- Going Through Tough Times
- Handling Conflict
- How to Make Great Choices
- Peer Pressure
- Succeeding in School
- The Bible and Me
- What's a Christian?
- Why God Made Me

The Youth Bible
The Bible to use with Faith 4 Life.

Visit your local Christian bookstore,
or contact Group Publishing, Inc., at 800-447-1070.
www.grouppublishing.com